MEN ARE WRITE

Jamaur Barnes | Jarrid Harris

Men Are Write
© 2023 Jamaur Barnes and Jarrid Harris
ISBN: 979-8-218-27896-0

Publishing Consultant: Mama's Kitchen Press
mamaskitchenpress.com

First Trade Paperback Original Edition, 2023

All rights reserved. No part of this publication may be reproduced, distributed, or transmitted in any form or by any means, including photocopying, recording, or other electronic or mechanical methods, without the prior written permission of the publisher, except in the case of brief quotations embodied in critical reviews and certain other noncommercial uses permitted by copyright law.

Printed in the United States of America

Edited by Camari Carter Hawkins
Cover Design and Layout Design by Krystle May Statler

Men Are Write is a bold, unapologetic journey of self-exploration, honesty, and an introspective walk down the hallway that is each man's mind! This interactive journal takes men of all ages on a journey of self-exploration, rediscovery, unpacking, accountability, and introspective thought, all while embracing and finding the simple joys of day-to-day life.

Journal, scribble, draw, reflect, craft—allow yourself to open up and meet the latest version of you! Each man will learn that there is no wrong way to meet himself; in fact, every way is the "write" way!

Think about the word "Man," and write down the first ten things that come to mind.
Why did you choose those ten words?

**and what made you cry?
How'd you feel afterward?**

Many times, self-reflection can uncover so many truths;
the first step in truth is acknowledgment.
How do you see yourself? How would you like others to see you?

How do you define love?
Does the way you define love stem from how you show love?

Where are you in reference to your dreams being fulfilled?

9

If you could go back to the past and change one thing about your life, what would you change and why?

A growth mindset means that you thrive on challenges and don't see failure as a way to describe yourself but as a springboard for growth and developing your abilities. A fixed mindset is when people see their qualities as fixed traits that cannot change.

Do you have a Growth or Fixed Mindset?
What can you do to enhance the mindset that you already have?

> "MINDSET IS 80% OF THE WAY THAT YOU PROCESS AND INTERPRET WHAT HAPPENS TO YOU ON A DAILY BASIS."
>
> — Jarrid Harris

Imagine that you get to have a conversation with someone that you've been estranged from or a person whom you wish you had a better relationship with. Write out how you'd like the conversation to go. What would you say? What would you like to hear from the other person?

If you do not have a consistent routine, take this time and create one below!

**When was the last time you genuinely said: "I love you"?
Who did you say it to, and how did their response make you feel?**

**How can you commit to being more present
and an active participant in your family?**

Write down the name of one person in your immediate family that you should have a better relationship with:

Write out three things that you are committed to carrying out to enhance your relationship with that person.

Nadir is described as the "lowest point in the fortunes of a person or organization." Think back on your "nadir," or lowest point. What was your biggest takeaway and/or something that you are grateful for from that time?

Walk to the mirror. Look at yourself. How do you see yourself?

Today, use the space below to write or create anything.

> "THUS ALSO FAITH BY ITSELF, IF IT DOES NOT HAVE WORKS, IS DEAD."
>
> James 2:17

Describe the last time you put your "faith" behind your "works, and what were the result(s)?

Trees are rooted beings that generally last for a very long time and are often difficult to move. People can often be our "trees," being strong "rooted" individuals who help and support our lives. Who is the strongest "tree" in your life?

Most kids grow up with a favorite superhero who has a specific superpower. Who is your real-life superhero, and what is their superpower? Why is that person your hero?

You learn more in failure than you ever would in success.
What is the last lesson that you learned from a failure?

What is the one memory that you hold on to that gets you through tough or difficult times?

**In what areas of your life have you hesitated to let others in?
What has made you reluctant to be open?**

Write down a truth that has been challenging for you to face or accept.

Write down your biggest secret. How does that secret make you feel?

"THE SECRET TO IMPROVING YOUR LIFE IS NOT FOCUSING ON THE OLD, BUT BUILDING BRICK-BY-BRICK ON THE NEW!"

Unknown

**How have you recovered from heartbreak or disappointment?
What is the best way to recover?
Could you have taken a healthier route?**

Who is the one person who knows you better than or just as much as you know yourself? What is some healthy feedback they would give you about yourself?

When was the last time you held another man accountable for his actions? What did you hold him accountable for?

If today was your last day and you had one last call to make, who would you call, and what would the conversation be?

40

When was the last time another man held you accountable for your actions, and what was he holding you accountable for?

Imagine that you were in need. Who are 3 to 5 people you would trust to encircle, encourage, protect, and or cover you? Next to each name, write a quality that indicates why that person made your list.

Where do you think your urges for procrastination originate from? What are some things that you generally procrastinate about? Write action items or plans to help eliminate your procrastination.

What is the most interesting and/or complex thing about you?

When was the last time you gave thanks, and what were you thankful for?

> "APOLOGIES CAN BE LIKE MEDICINE: HEALING, AFFIRMING, RESOLVING."
>
> — Unknown

**Write a letter to someone to who you owe an apology.
You can also write an apology letter to yourself.**

Write about a time you were grateful something didn't happen. What lesson did you take from this experience?

50

Oftentimes, we show others appreciation and forget to acknowledge and celebrate ourselves. How do you show yourself appreciation?

**about your day with genuine concern?
How did it make you feel?**

Men are not often celebrated in the ways we would like; we are often simply disregarded. What are ways that men could be appreciated more?

On a separate sheet of paper, write a letter to someone that you have yet to forgive. Afterward, burn, shred, or discard the letter.

"OFTENTIMES, FREEDOM IS ON THE OTHER SIDE OF WHAT WE ARE REFUSING TO LET GO OF. FREEDOM IS OFTEN RIGHT AT OUR FINGERTIPS, YET WE REFUSE TO GRASP IT."

Unknown

59

French = merci • Spanish = gracias • German = danke
Italian = grazie • Portuguese = obrigado • Chinese = xièxiè
Hindi/Indian = dhanyavaad • Farsi/Persian = mamnoon
"Thank You" can sound and be interpreted differently.
How do you process "thank you" when it's genuinely said to you?
How does it make you feel?

"What's up?" • "You Good?"
"What's good?" • "What's going on?"
We often greet each other as a formality in passing but don't always mean what we say or stop to sit in the conversation.
When was the last time someone genuinely checked in with you, and how did it make you feel?

The age old saying, "You can't judge a book by its cover," has been repeated time and time again. Oftentimes, the worth of a man is equated to the value of what he can contribute externally. What are some internal things about yourself that people may often overlook?

Self-care is the process of taking care of yourself with behaviors that promote health and active management of illness when it occurs. Self-care can be found in food choices, exercise, sleep, mental health care, time for yourself, and more!
When was the last time you took time
for "self-care"? How did it make you feel?

Men are often seen as "one-dimensional" beings, our feelings and thoughts are not always considered. What are thoughts you have that others might be surprised to hear or know?

Oftentimes, men are expected to be the "Rock," the "Caregiver," the "Provider," the "Understanding One," the "Nurturer." If you, as a man, are expected to be those things, who are those things for you?

What in your life needs to change? Draft a plan and immediate goals for you to start working toward today that will enhance your life.

Write as many positive things about yourself as you can.
What did you learn from this activity?

> "LIFE IS ABOUT DONATION, NOT DURATION."

Unknown

**When was the last time you gave back?
How can you give back today?**

Shadow Work: Working with your unconscious mind to uncover the parts of yourself that you hide from yourself. This can include trauma or parts of your personality that you subconsciously consider undesirable. Write about something that others may not know about you that you are aware needs improvement.

Many times, men don't tap into our feelings because they are seen as weak. Close your eyes and think about the word "feelings." "Brain dump" below, and write down a list of feelings you battle with or thoughts you have about the word "feelings." Afterward, circle or highlight things you would like to lean more into.

Men wear several hats and have several assignments, oftentimes saying "Yes" too much, forgetting to say "No." The word "No" is a full sentence. Write a list of things you need to say "No" to.

At this point in your life, are you where you thought you would be? Why or why not? If you are not where you'd like to be, what steps can you take to get there?

Men often have the mindset, "I have to make it happen–no excuses," and many of us want most things "right now!" Write about a recent time when you exercised your patience, sat, and allowed something to "just happen."

> 'Character,' like a home, is built brick by brick, with the finished product being a grand structure—a work of art! What phase in your life helped build your character?

> "THE ROOT OF GRATITUDE IS 'ATTITUDE.' THE QUALITY OF BEING THANKFUL; READINESS TO SHOW APPRECIATION FOR AND TO RETURN KINDNESS TO SOMEONE."
>
> Unknown

How do you express your anger? Has the way you express your anger helped you to be a better man or stood in the way of your growth?

Write a list of things that make up your self-identity or the way you see yourself. How honest was this list of things that you wrote down?

Rank these things in order of importance: Family, Money, Intimacy, Love, Self, Health, God (or Religion), Community, Success, Knowledge (or Education). Next, write about why you ranked these categories in the order you did.

Does your identity derive from your life experiences? Does your identity equate to the person you would like to be in the next 5 years? Why? What is the most significant experience that you've had that has shaped who you are at this very moment?

If someone had 30 seconds to explain who you are as a person, what would they say?

85

Pride can be a gift and a curse. How does pride play a factor in your life? Does your pride serve you, or does it work against you?

Fill in the following and expand the thought:
If it wasn't for _____, I wouldn't be _____...

List three people who are highly influential to you. Why did each person make your list?

89

"YOU HAVE TO HAVE THE CAPACITY AND THE ABILITY TO TAKE WHAT PEOPLE DID, AND HOW THEY DID IT, AND FORGIVE THEM AND MOVE ON."

John Lewis

Have you been having faith and not working toward a specific thing, or have you been working toward a specific thing and not having faith?

93

Optimism is the belief that things will work out and the confidence that situations will yield the most positive results. Pessimism is the thought process that most or some things will not work out, and situations will likely yield negative results.
What area in your life are you most pessimistic about, and how could you change your mindset to be more optimistic?

Complacency is defined as a feeling of quiet pleasure or security, often while unaware of some potential danger, defect, or the like; self-satisfaction or smug satisfaction with an existing situation, condition, etc. What are you most complacent about? Where does your complacency stem from?

What unique characteristic or ability sets you apart from others?

What characteristic of yours has led to your success thus far?

In detail, describe the driving factor(s) in your quest for success.

What part of yourself could you die a little bit more to in order to be happier?

100

> "DYING TO YOURSELF IS ACTUALLY THE BEGINNING OF LIVING."
>
> — J.D. Stanley

**Who in your life believes in you the most?
What is it about you that makes them believe?**

Men often praise the traits of others and do not always take time to appreciate and praise themselves. What is the most admirable trait about yourself?

**Healing does not often happen overnight.
Healing can be a process, a journey.
What area of your life could you use a little more healing in?**

What about you might be a shock for others to learn?

How does your life serve as an example to others?

After getting to know you, what strengths would someone say shine through most?

Are you who you are because of what you believe, or are you who you are because of what others have said about you or told you?

109

What part of you should you share more with others?

What do you need more of as a man, and from who or where?

"WRITE THE VISION, AND MAKE IT PLAIN UPON TABLES, THAT HE MAY RUN THAT READETH IT. FOR THE VISION IS YET FOR AN APPOINTED TIME, BUT AT THE END, IT SHALL SPEAK, AND NOT LIE: THOUGH IT TARRY, WAIT FOR IT; BECAUSE IT WILL SURELY COME, IT WILL NOT TARRY."

Habbakuh 2:2-3

Write a vision of where you see your life in the next 12 months. What steps will you take to keep yourself encouraged and accountable about your vision?

**Intuition: an ability to understand or know something without needing to think about it or use reason to discover it.
Reflect on a time you ignored your intuition. What was the result?**

"Masks" can serve to hide identities, feelings, and emotions.
As men, we can wear many masks to hide many things.
When was the last time you masked something?

Transparently write about how you're feeling today.

Take a moment to reflect. What do you owe yourself?

Frustration is a natural emotion that we all feel; at times, our frustration converts to anger; and sometimes, we act in ways that we either don't want or are unhealthy. When you are frustrated or angry, what is a healthy way to handle your emotions?

Indulge means to yield to the desire of; to treat with excessive leniency, generosity, or consideration; to give free rein to; to take unrestrained pleasure in; to gratify. What are some healthy habits you indulge in that enhance or add value to your life?

Write down one or more habits that may be holding you back from becoming a better version of yourself. Afterward, be honest with yourself: Write down how you can detach from this/those habit(s).

Write down the names of three men that you care most about. Call those three men and speak encouraging and uplifting words to them. At the conclusion of the call, challenge each man to do the same.

What are you most hopeful about?

> "FAITH IS THE SUBSTANCE OF THINGS HOPED FOR, THE EVIDENCE OF THINGS NOT SEEN."
>
> Hebrews 11:1 KJV

When was the last time you felt discouraged, and how did you react?

How have you evolved in the past twelve months?

How do you see yourself as a man?
Fill in the space below with your personal reflections.

Write a list of things you'd like to see for yourself in the next five years. How will you accomplish things on that list?

"A loss is not always a loss, it's often a lesson."
What is the last loss that turned into a lesson for you?
What did you learn?

Men often do not take time to recognize or celebrate themselves. Write about something you need to recognize or celebrate yourself for.

**Pick three words that describe you at this moment in your life.
What do these words represent about you?**

What is something you've always wanted to do but didn't because you were afraid others would judge you for?

If you could change anything about your life right now, what would it be? Why have you not made such change(s) before today?

What is the best piece of advice you've ever received?
How did that advice impact you?

"GRAY AREAS ARE OFTEN PLACES OR SPOTS IN OUR LIFE WHERE MORE CLARITY OR UNDERSTANDING IS NEEDED, AND WE DON'T HAVE IT. THUS, THEY CAN CREATE 'FOGGY,' OR CONFUSING SPACES."

— Jamaur Barnes

Write about a "gray" area in your life and what steps you can take to make it more "clear."

Take a moment to reflect on who you were ten years ago;
write a letter to the person you were. What would you have shared
with yourself then that would help you to be the best you today?

If you could have a transparent conversation with your parent(s) at any time in your life, past or present, when would that time be, and what would you say?

Second-guessing yourself can be a form of self-sabotage. When we second guess ourselves, we often tell ourselves lies that can impact our confidence or the way that we see ourselves. In what area or areas of your life have you been second-guessing yourself?

2 Ways to address the challenging areas
1 Change You Hope to See from this exercise

Who are you when no one is watching?

140

How do you measure failure? How do you measure success?

About the Authors

JAMAUR BARNES

Jamaur Barnes is a Tacoma, Washington born but Houston, Texas raised Community Developer, with a passion for people and serving through joy! Driven by the mission of, "Nothing for us, without us," he holds tight to the mission that each project should be created with and for its intended audience, which is just how, "Men are Write" came to be! Realizing the market for tools on mental health for men (particularly Black men) is narrow at best, he knows this work will explode pathways and close mental and emotional gaps all at once, for men everywhere.

The retired but decorated educator, and now Entrepreneur and Philanthropist draws from his experience with Black men and youth, coupled with his own upbringing as fuel to drive the vehicle that is his first co-authored work. The Prairie View A&M University graduate and member of Alpha Phi Alpha Fraternity, Incorporated, hopes that each man sees himself in the pages of this book, all while meeting the latest version of himself—a version that he will be bold enough to share with others and continue to develop within himself!

JARRID HARRIS

Jarrid Harris, a proud alumnus of Prairie View A&M University, holds a Bachelor of Business Administration degree in Marketing. Since 2019, he has thrived as a sales consultant in the wine and spirits industry. Originally from New Orleans, Louisiana, Jarrid relocated to Houston in the aftermath of Hurricane Katrina.

Harris is an active and dedicated member of Alpha Phi Alpha Fraternity, Incorporated, where he has held the roles of Vice President and committee member. Driven by a profound commitment to nurturing the potential of young minds, he finds fulfillment in mentoring. He aims to channel this passion through his nonprofit initiative, 'F.L.Y. Standards' (Fulfilling the Lives of Youth), and is actively developing 'The Harris Hopes Project.'

Over the years, Jarrid has extended mentorship to the youth through various organizations, including his fraternity, the 100 Black Men of America, Metropolitan Houston, and the Collegiate 100 at Prairie View A&M University. In each capacity, his overarching mission has remained consistent: to foster meaningful connections, make a positive impact, and empower those whom he is fortunate enough to cross paths with."

> "HEALING DOES NOT OFTEN HAPPEN OVERNIGHT. HEALING CAN BE A PROCESS, A JOURNEY."
>
> — Unknown

www.ingramcontent.com/pod-product-compliance
Lightning Source LLC
Chambersburg PA
CBRC091208010526
44107CB00022B/1263